Heartdates

Heartdates

Reflections on Life

Ina Timmer

Jane & Skip
Hope you enjoy
Ina

iUniverse, Inc.
New York Lincoln Shanghai

Heartdates
Reflections on Life

iUniverse books may be ordered through booksellers or by contacting:

iUniverse
2021 Pine Lake Road, Suite 100
Lincoln, NE 68512
www.iuniverse.com
1-800-Authors (1-800-288-4677)

ISBN-13: 978-0-595-42198-5 (pbk)
ISBN-13: 978-0-595-86536-9 (ebk)
ISBN-10: 0-595-42198-9 (pbk)
ISBN-10: 0-595-86536-4 (ebk)

Printed in the United States of America

To:
My husband, Dave, for his daring,
my children, Christine and Tony, for their caring,
and my sister, Ada, for her sharing.

A special thank you to Tony Copeland
for his beautiful artwork.

Contents

Creation

The universe, delighting in creation,
Gasped with pleasure at its latest thought,
And in one giant, bursting exhalation,
Pronounced the Word, and all the world was wrought.

You

It isn't what you're wearing,
Or the color of your hair,
It's not your gold and silver
That make people aware,
It's the way your eyes are shining,
And the way your face just glows,
It's the way you're always smiling,
It's the love inside, that shows.

Choices

Choices tell the living tale of each of our life's sum,
Of what we were, and what we are and what we will become,
Choices are what set us forth on our particular way,
Sometimes the only choice to take is what our elders say.

However, there must come a time we take ourselves in hand,
When we decide what's right for us and when we take our stand,
For soon or late there comes a point where do is what we must,
Remaining indecisive leaves us standing in the dust.

And so we check the roads, we ponder, push or sit a spell,
Then off we go, and what's beyond, choices and time will tell.
Not always green, not always bliss, not always sunny skies,
Sometimes a desert parched, a pain intense within us lies.

We make a turn, we forge ahead, and yes, we could be wrong,
Mistakes, regrets, indulgences, we know we should be strong.
Our lives a layer of choices building one upon the next,
A blend of all we've done and said until we have our text.

With cover worn we read our tale, and hope that others too,
Have been at least a little helped by what we chose to do,
That they've felt loved and understood, believing in our care
In making choices that were good for all of us to share.

One Way or the Other

It's attitude, perception, the way we look at life,
That paves our road with inner peace,
Or scatters it with strife,
In action or reaction, we flow or we rebel,
We're tossed about on stormy seas,
Or learn to anchor well,
In any situation, we always have the choice,
To face our foes with loving hearts,
Or give our fears a voice.

The Looking Glass

Birds in cages, all for sale,
Feathered rainbows locked in jail,
Cries for help to set them free,
To be all they used to be.
Wolves behind a chain link fence,
Stand and stare, then recommence
Pacing, back and forth they go,
While we watch the wildlife show.
Leopards, beauty behind glass,
Aimless lives, usefulness past,
Black bears, rhythmically swaying,
Innocent generations paying.
With the animals extinct
And ourselves a vital link,
Will we be the next rare breed,
Will some stronger force succeed?
Will we, at the very last,
Pace and stare, behind the glass?

Music in my Blood

The music's in my blood, it's in my blood, it's in my bones,
The rhythm and the beat and all the glorious, glorious tones,
With rainbow coloured skirt, stiletto heels I twirl around,
Hands clapping, fingers snapping, feet that hardly touch the ground.
The music's in our blood, it's in our breath, it's in the air,
It's bringing folks together, people dancing everywhere.
We shimmy and we shake, we razzle dazzle on the floor,
We laugh, we sing, we glide, we swing, then boogey out the door.
The music's in our blood, we snake our way on down the street,
A swaying, pirouetting line, oh my, oh my, it's sweet,
Wild hair a swinging, voices ringing, bouncing up and down,
With music in our blood, we wend our way and wake the town!

In the Shade of the Old Oak Tree

While walking through the forest I looked up to meet a tree,
I wanted to learn wisdom that it held inherently,
To learn about it's steadfast strength and ever-present calm,
To feel it's penetrating peace pierce through me with its balm,
Its leafy arms reached skyward in perpetual, joyous prayer,
In knowledge that it's God is all around it, everywhere.
My hand followed the roots that disappeared into the earth,
My arms reached round to feel the warming comfort of its girth.
And in the shelter of its branches forest life abounds,
I sat beneath in wonder, listening to the forest sounds.
The tree and wind together played a soothing melody,
Singing the songs of nature in its sweet simplicity.

More Than We Seem

Water, content to be water,
Equally nice, being ice,
And can't resist, rising into mist,
Seeming to disappear,
Then reappear,
As clouds, like hovering shrouds,
Falling again,
As rain,
Joining itself,
Becoming teams,
That flow in streams,
A change once more,
To waves upon the shore.

Familiar Stirrings

As spring peeps shyly through the snow,
And buds plump rounded fill the woods,
And air is filled once more with song,
I know it's time for me to go.

The old familiar stirring starts,
A restless rhythm through the years,
The calling of an unknown place,
Clamps firmly round my ready heart.

The wind will lead me, where, who knows,
The trees my shade, my rest, my bed,
Well cleansed by rain, warmed by the sun,
I'll follow where the warm breeze blows.

Second Chance

I never really knew him till the end,
Only then, I recognized my friend,
His weakness was the key to my closed heart,
The gentle strength in him tore me apart.

Amazed I was, so many folks dropped by,
They loved him; there were many reasons why,
A dinner here, a helping hand out there,
He cared for all, it was himself he'd share.

He said he didn't wish to be alone,
And so I stayed, not daring to go home,
Sleeping most nights right there beside his bed,
Not wanting to miss any word he said.

One early morning with spring in the air,
I woke and knew he was no longer there,
His soul had found its freedom in the night,
His spirit seeking, soaring to the light.

A learning time, those days of tragedy,
A pondering time of what is meant to be,
Impossible to measure each life's worth,
We all must live our fullest here on earth.

Purpose

Flowers, sharing with all,
Blooming wherever the seeds fall,
Never discriminating, always giving,
Knowing their purpose and reason,
For living.

An Enchanted Night

It feels like I could walk that path of moonlight,
And thus explore the wonders of the sea,
I'd tiptoe lightly on the shimmering water,
I'd laugh and sing so elfin-like and free.

I'd dance with whales and fishes and the dolphins,
They'd play and twirl beside my path of light,
I'd kneel down very gently to caress them,
Then slide upon their backs, and we'd take flight.

We'd frolic with our friends throughout the ocean,
Our guardian whitely glowing overhead,
We'd celebrate and sing till early morning,
Before returning sleepily to bed.

I'd say so long back by my silver highway,
And walk to shore before the break of dawn,
I'd turn around and wave to my companions,
And watch until the last of them had gone.

Was I just standing on the shore and dreaming,
Was it perhaps a giddy, surreal swoon?
Or was I really dancing with the dolphins,
Bedazzled by that ancient, glorious moon?

Reaching Out

Come, hold my hand, reach out to forge a chain,
And in the holding, I myself, am held again,
Not only held, but healed, the wounds between us closed,
Becoming friends, no longer fearful foes.
Here, take my hand, love's offered with this clasp,
Comfort and hope, for you and me within its grasp.

The Lady Fisherwoman

A little femininity amongst the mostly male,
Palapa roof for shade to keep that fragile shade of pale,
She's mending nets with hands worn rough and veined
With signs of age,
Her glasses perched upon her nose, she's nodding like a sage.
She's quite a lady, in a rough and tumble kind of place,
Her bright red nails a touch of class, a smile upon her face.

For forty years she's lived a life barren of luxuries,
But coiffed and curled, she still exudes a sense of fun and ease.
With worn and sun bleached couch, and shanty hut
Upon the dunes,
She works beside her husband as she hums her native tunes.

Cont'd

And just before the dusk, before the sun begins to set,
She helps him drag the boat to sea
And there they cast their net.
She hauls the fish and guts the catch, his helper and his mate,
But back on shore, she uses much a different sort of bait.

For when the sun has gone and in the moon's romantic glow,
The hair, the nails, become the setting for a different show.
The battered couch is now a bed, a lovers rendezvous,
Under the stars she holds him close, as they begin to woo.

This is her life, her man, her home, her own particular way,
The lady fisherwoman whom we met
Along the bay.

Rediscovery

Innocence, trust, unconditional love,
We are born to this world,
With these gifts from above,
But then we forget, or we lose, or we bury
Our treasures,
In anger, in fear and in worry,
Then spend all our lives digging deep for what's lost,
At such great expense, such incredible cost,
Attracted to glitter and glory and praise,
Forgetting the purpose,
For which we were raised.
It takes us a lifetime of struggle and pain,
To come back full circle to childhood again,
Innocence, trust, unconditional love,
Rediscovered, remembered, restored from above.

A Soft Goodbye

You've disappeared, gone, vanished,
I couldn't say goodbye,
Too far away, no time, too late,
You must have known I'd try.
I wonder, were you calling?
Needing a hand to hold?
I would have clasped yours to my breast,
Kept it from growing cold.
So much I longed to be there,
Not wishing you alone,
And prayed you felt love all around,
As you were traveling home.

I think you heard me weeping,
And sent a sign to show,
You'd gone to somewhere greater yet,
You had to let me know.
An owl, never had one been seen,
In that particular wood,
Swooped past and settled on a branch
As quietly I stood,
We shared a gaze of healing,
My heavy heart grew light,
In freedom and with ease, the owl,
Flew softly out of sight.

At Last, Fulfilled

It's like a part of me came home the day we met,
A part I hadn't really known I'd lost, and yet
An emptiness was always there inside,
A yearning longing I had tried to hide.

You sparked within me feelings that had dormant lain,
And so rekindled embers of my life again,
Now all the joys of an eternity,
And all its wonders too, return to me.

Long have I walked this path of still despair,
Finding it simpler to no longer care.
Using a nonchalance as my disguise,
Smiling, to hide the void behind my eyes.

You blew the flames of life back to my heart,
And found the prodigal piece, that vital part
Long missing from the well within my soul,
You found that part, and made me whole.

Oh, Sister!

Whatever can one say about a sister,
When growing up I never really missed her,
Sharing a room invisibly divided,
She on her side, and I on mine abided.

Her problems and her friends to me were strangers,
As mostly were her dreams, her hopes, her dangers,
Her interests not at all the same as mine,
We didn't stop to share a lot of time.

Now looking back we clearly see our treasure,
Togetherness today a valued pleasure,
That bedroom surely would have been so bare,
Without my older sister being there.

Golden Olden Friends

Don't think our friendship has an end,
And I no longer care,
Don't judge my silences a sign,
Of nothing left to share.
Don't let seeming indifference
Take a hold within your heart,
Allowing bitter thoughts to drive
Us even more apart.
Delight in memories of old,
Embrace the glasses raised,
Remember us the way we were,
The warmth of olden days.
For time and circumstance take hold,
They lead down separate roads,
And distance leads to silence
As we bear our separate loads.
But in between the living
In between the daily bread,
I think upon your face,
And take it gently to my bed.

Ode to 911

When men think more of power and wealth,
And use religion as disguise,
When gaining ground and waging war,
Are seen as logical and wise.

When countless lives and families,
Are shattered, torn beyond repair,
Then we are lost in darkness deep,
For we have lost the will to care.

But if a few can hold the light,
A few can hope, and waiver not,
If they to evil will not bend,
And standing firm will not be bought.

Then slowly, surely, love will prove,
It's power o'er all, its shining grace,
We'll recognize we're brothers all,
One family called the human race.

There is an urgency, a need,
To mend the rifts in history,
To reach across the chasms vast,
A giant bridge to set us free.

Cont'd

We need to join hands one with one,
Linking our hearts, not locking heads,
We need to unlock chains of steel,
Start forging chains of love instead.

There's still a chance for us to learn,
To understand the other's view,
If we could close our eyes, and feel,
The things that other person knew.

And in the feeling realize,
That deep within we're all the same,
No need to differentiate,
No need to find someone to blame.

Let's "love our neighbour as ourselves",
Leave hate and prejudice behind,
A bond of prayer connecting all,
Lighting the world for humankind.

Eternal Quest

What is the meaning behind all religion,
What is it that we're all striving towards?
Why do we gather in temples and churches,
The longing in each that strikes the same chord?
Is it a yearning for something not concrete,
A feeling, a reaching for something unseen?
A sense of belonging, a spiritual bonding
Returning to places our souls have once been?

What Really Matters

Our fires may not gleam as bright,
Our stride not quite as long,
Our aim not be as steady,
And our stroke not half as strong,
But the embers glowing in our hearts,
The strength that grows within,
The wisdom winding through our years,
The peace that age can bring,
Are all the prize we ever need,
The trophies we desire,
The lessons learned through tears and joy,
All fuel an ageless fire.

Child's Play

What did you do as a child,
What brought you the greatest joy,
What made the minutes and hours fly by,
What was your favorite toy?

Was it the books that you read,
Or maybe a walk in the wild,
Was there a particular game you recall
With bliss, when you were a child?

It's through recollections like these,
We find the right path to pursue,
By wiping away the layers of dust,
We reveal the bright child we once knew.

Everywhere

I see God's face in my garden,
I hear God's voice by the shore,
In the sweet caress of a breeze on my face,
I feel God's presence once more.

In the gentleness of the sunrise,
In the gathering of a storm,
In an acorn grown to a mighty oak,
The power of God is born.

God sings a song through the blackbird,
And dances on butterfly wings,
In the fragrant scent of a summer rose,
Is the healing that only God brings.

All the Wrong Places

I looked for heaven here and there,
For meaning I looked everywhere,
Town after town, book after book,
I searched and read and looked and looked.
I asked the folks I chanced upon,
Did they know where the truth had gone,
Had they seen heaven passing by,
Had they once heard its glorious cry?
But no one knew and no one shared,
And in their hurry, no one cared,
So on I searched and at the last,
There was nobody left to ask.
My questing finally took me home,
Back to my childhood, where alone
And in the stillness of the glade,
A realization deep I made.
My bliss was never to be found,
In other folks or other towns,
The answer, with me from the start,
Patiently waited, in my heart.

A Different Road

Let me be not judge of others,
Nor indifferent to another,
Let me see, not just with eyes
But with heart, past each disguise,
Let me feel another's sadness,
And rejoice with them in gladness,
Share their burden and their sorrow,
Help them reach out for tomorrow,
Let my self be humble, knowing
That the road they now are going,
Might be mine if life unraveled,
And a different road I traveled.

Aged Dilemma

Carefully led, properly fed,
Old man sitting on his bed,
Listlessly facing days ahead.
Are we kind or are we blind,
A huge octogenarian bind,
Is it cruel, and are we fools,
Have we broken all the rules.
Bodies kept whole, killing soul,
Is longevity the goal?
Down the hall an anguished call,
Another aged body falls.
A pressing sense, despair immense,
Pervading loneliness intense.
A little tug, a need to hug,
A giant, living tomb we've dug.
What's to be done, this aging crew
Has somehow multiplied, and grew
So fast, how can this last,
Increasingly a bigger task.
Can what's begun, still be undone,
Can these old souls still find the sun,
Is this a race that can be won?

Just Do It!

I worried just a bit at first,
And wondered if I should,
I wondered if the time was right,
And if I really could.

I fussed about the timing,
And I fretted over stuff,
And endlessly went round and round,
Until I'd had enough.

But then I started right back in,
And with a vengeance, thought,
That this was not the thing to do,
That I'd be surely caught.

I'd jump into the middle,
And would sink right out of sight,
I'd lose all I had gained,
And then would have to up and fight.

Cont'd

It wouldn't work, a big mistake,
Better to shut it down,
This silly plan, a crazy scheme,
For certain I would drown.

In all the vague uncertainties,
And little known terrain,
In unfamiliar circumstance,
What can I really gain?

And then a giddy feeling,
A warm quiver in my heart,
Was telling me to venture forth
And urging me to start.

It said that there is not a time
That's better than the rest,
The time is now, it's here, it's come,
It's asking for my best.

Frog Frolic

Frogs, itty bitty things,
Would you say a frog sings
Or does he scream, or does he yell,
Whatever it's called, he does it well.
He and his cousins,
Dozens and dozens,
Singing a chorus from dusk till four,
Hearty frog songs of Froggian lore,
Through summer and fall,
The great Todos Santos Frog Call.

Winged Imaginings

I sat myself down on the edge of a bank,
And dreamily gazed at the sky,
The wisps and the curls of the clouds sailed by,
And I pictured myself flying high.
I'd be flying across a weightless sky,
I'd be diving and swooping with ease,
I'd spread out my arms like a pair of wings,
And glide gracefully on the breeze.
My feathery friends would flock all about,
They'd ask me to join in their fun,
We'd choreograph a bird ballet,
On a floating stage under the sun.
We'd decorate it with cottony clouds,
And a rainbow arched over the top,
With a sky the colors of azure and pink,
To serve as a fitting backdrop.
A saucy, light wind would announce the show,
In formation, we'd make our debut,
Feathers well preened, hearts bursting with song,
Soaring higher than ever we flew.
My body may perch on the edge of a bank,
It has no visible wings,
But that doesn't stop me from flying away,
To partake in most wondrous things.

Ourselves To Blame

If we keep ourselves hardened and cold,
We might do very well, growing old,
We may think life is grand
Give ourselves a big hand,
To have not become caught in the fold.

If relationships always go wrong,
And we see our indifference as strong,
Then we'll build a great wall
For support ere we fall,
Give ourselves not a chance to belong.

We may feel we do well with a heart
Shriveled into the size of a dart,
Shooting arrows of blame
A sadistical game,
Guaranteed it will keep us apart.

Till at last, at the end, we're alone,
With a heart that has turned into stone,
Not a tear is there shed,
Not one loving word said,
Too late then, to forgive and atone.

Wasted Dreams

I've defeated my heart, she said,
And brought it under control,
I've carefully mapped out my future plans,
And know how they play a role.
I've organized all my dreams,
Safely tucked them into a drawer,
I take them out every now and again
To dream what I dreamt once before.
With time they have grown more dim,
Their luster has faded away,
Now seldom do I even open the drawer,
In the sameness of day after day.
Yet sometimes inside me, a voice,
Determined it is to be heard,
In the still of the night when my soul will not sleep,
It persists in repeating this word.

Cont'd

"Dream, dream, dream," does it shout!
For your purpose, your bliss lies there,
"Dream," as all people are meant to do,
Have faith and the courage to dare!
Fling open that place in your heart,
Sweep fears of the unknown aside,
Live the dream that once had you singing your song,
Shake it loose, know there's nothing to hide!
The outcome is not what's at stake,
The way it turns out matters not,
But time running out with your bliss not begun,
Is something that must be fought,
Take the path that you know to be true,
And don't ever think it's too late,
At the end of the journey that follows your heart,
Lies the dream only you can create.

You Never Know

Be humble, kind and wise,
For God is often in disguise,
And when we fail to know His face,
And recognize him not,
It's each other we've forgot.

My World

There's many a path up the mountain,
With many a detour too,
Diversions there are aplenty,
To keep us from carrying through.

There's many a reason for stopping,
Excuses at every turn,
There's really no reason for trying,
Just what are we here to learn?

Why can't I meander and dawdle
Sit down and admire the view?
Why should I be always striving,
What am I supposed to do?

Yet as I gaze out from my viewpoint,
My eyes catch distressing sights,
There are children starving in Africa,
Disease, epidemics and blights.

cont'd

Over there I can see people fighting,
The screams of the women are clear.
An abandoned child reaches out his hand
And pleads, but does anyone hear?

In the distance, smog blots the horizon,
Pollution and garbage piled high,
The river wades sluggishly through it,
And all the animals die.

My indifference turns into discomfort,
Embarrassment nudges my heart,
I had no particular agenda,
Now, I don't know quite where to start.

But a start is the step to beginning,
And beginning's the start of the way,
I'm meant to carry my share of life,
It's my world, I'm obliged to pay.

A Common Humanity

You, on your side, and I on mine,
I have my tea, you have your wine,
I'm fresh and showered, you're barely there,
I feel empowered, you need a chair.
I in my smugness, don't see at all,
Your signs of struggle to halt your fall,
Your resignation to reality,
Your ups and downs, your silent plea.
I know nothing of your grief and strife,
Nor do you know my way in life.
A common moment has made us friends,
Our difference fades, the edges blend,
Just people, working side by side,
Helping another, is our guide,
Disparate though our backgrounds be,
Does anything separate you from me?

The Running Shoe Tree

The road runs through a lone, distant place,
Of very little beauty and even less grace,
The land is barren and the hills show their bones,
The wind whistles loud, in shrill overtones.

In this desolation a phenomenon stands,
A tree festooned with unusual garlands.
Not leaves or feathers, nor paper or flags,
No ribbons bedeck this gnarled silver snag.

But running shoes, tied to each other with laces
And flung over branches in various places!
Clusters of runners like some foreign fruit,
Ripe for the picking, this well heeled loot!

Hundreds had fallen, soiled, bruised and worn,
A season of canvas and rubber, now torn.
A running shoe tree, such a welcome surprise,
So rare, I could hardly believe my eyes!

Legacy

While seeking my own answers,
Did I raise questions for you?
In filling my emptiness
Did your own doubts come through,
Are your uncertainties a reflection of mine,
Do I see my fears in your eyes shine,
Did my weakness stain your heart,
My sorrows, also tear you apart?
Or have you become stronger,
More able to bend,
Perhaps more resilient,
Much lighter, a friend
To yourself, someone who can see
Not bound, but immensely more free,
Willing to forgive and forget,
To live day by day and to bet
On your life, and your talent,
To be kind to yourself, and gallant.

Dad

He's sitting out here on the bench,
Sun shining gently on his head,
Eyes closed, he's in his own dream world,
And hasn't heard a word I've said.

More oft than not his heart takes flight,
And settles softly in a place,
Where, waiting patiently he knows,
He'll soon see loved ones face to face.

His body looks so old and frail,
It's disappearing day by day,
I want to wrap him in my arms,
To keep him from fading away.

It's me who isn't ready yet,
To see the spot that he'll leave bare,
I've loved him so through all these years,
And can't imagine him not there.

My Dad has always said to me,
That life and death are just as one,
Like stepping through an open door,
That leads right back where we've begun.

His years and mine are woven fast,
With threads of joy, and love, and pain,
My father, teacher, and my friend,
Forever bound, we'll meet again.

A Special Garden

If I could plant a garden of souls,
I'd do it with utmost care,
I'd furrow and till and rake the rows,
A fertile foundation prepare.
A mixture of tenderness, patience and faith
Would softly line their beds,
Caresses, blessings and kisses sweet,
I'd lay upon their heads,
I'd tuck them in gently, one by one,
And cover them over with love,
Then softly lull them to sleep with song,
Watched over by angels above.
Well watered by words of wisdom old,
From sages of long ago,
The air filled with sunshine and laughter and joy,
I'd watch those little souls grow.

Book of Generations

I, when in my youthful singularity,
Thought to make my stand alone, and free,
Caught in youth's grandeur and immortal rapture,
Not seeing, then, my life as added chapter.

My story, carrying on the book of generations,
Their story, laying down the path and its foundation,
Our story, blended tales of living history
Unfinished glimpse, of whom I've come to be.

Yourself, Myself

My wish for you is to see yourself,
The way that others do,
To recognize in warmth and grace,
Your spirit shining through,
To see your smile that melts a heart,
And see the light that you impart,
To really see yourself,
My wish for you.

My prayer for you is to know yourself,
And understand the way,
Emotions often take the lead,
And dictate what you say,
To know the why of joy and pain,
Forgive yourself time and again,
To know yourself,
That is my prayer for you.

cont'd

My hope for you is for gentleness,
For kindness to yourself,
To take your imperfections
Put them high up on the shelf,
Not dust them off and scrutinize
But learn from them, become more wise,
More kindness for yourself,
My hope for you.

My wishes, hopes and prayers for you,
Are just as much my own,
Reflecting all the things I do,
Remembering what I've known,
My wish for you is also mine,
To open wide and let love shine,
To know yourself, to know myself,
I pray.

Torn Apart

They say home is where the heart is,
And I believe that's true,
I find the hardest part is,
When the home is torn in two.

A Solitary Life

A ghostly figure in the mist I see
And wondering if it's you,
Or is it just my longing that you be,
That you are here, and more than memory.

Your gentle voice to hear again a spell,
As hand in hand we walk,
And bubbling over with so much to tell,
No one but you, knows me so very well.

Through thickened fog surely your face is there,
More than a trick mirage,
This ever widening gap so much to bear,
A tiring game this life of solitaire.

A weakened sun struggles to light the dawn,
To warm the world anew,
Slowly the mists and shrouds again withdrawn,
I turn to reach for you, but you are gone.

And the World Cries

Why do we feel the need to conquer,
Change and destroy whatever's in our way,
Why do we never stop to wonder
And listen to what nature has to say.
Why do we always think it's our right
To stake a claim but seldom stop to care,
Then plunder and pollute all that's around us,
Leave in our wake a trail that's dead and bare.
Are we so deaf believing just our own voice,
Are we so blind, around us we can't see,
Cocooned within our little self worlds,
Each focused solely on our selfish spree.
The earth laments our brazen folly,
It cries out from the forest floor,
It mourns its passing in the whale song,
It screams a message till it can no more.
And then the whole world will be silent,
No bird song will enthrall the sky,
No cry of coyote, no more wind sighs,
And nothing left of you and I.

The Healing Place

Let stillness fill your soul,
An instrument to make you whole,
Allow the quiet place within
To shut the world outside,
Let silence be your guide.

We enter silence weak,
We always feel the need to speak,
But then surrendering to the calm
And listening at great length,
We recognize our strength.

My Treasured Love

I'll plant you a garden to rest your soul,
Sweet bird songs will fill the air,
A rainbow of flowers as feast for your eyes,
And soft, fragrant grasses your chair.
The leafy lace shade of a friendly oak,
Caresses of warmth from the sun,
The evening's soft glow in the moon's mellow light,
My forever embrace when day's done.

Miracle You

A miracle of happiness, that's you,
A ray of golden sunshine in a sky of blue,
A rainbow on a cloudy day, a song to chase the sad away,
A dance, a smile stretching for miles,
That's you.

No Question

Once I went a walking,
On a path of tarry black,
I chanced upon a little bump,
The next day I went back.

A little shoot of green appeared,
Had pushed its way right through,
Determined twas to reach the light,
The only thing it knew.

No question of its aim,
So focused on the task,
Of doing what its purpose was,
It never stopped to ask.

A Priceless Reminder

It's easy to go through each day,
And never stop to think,
That each today is special,
Each today a golden link
That ties the past together
With our future days to be,
That lets us live and love and laugh,
And hopes that we will see,
The link of now, our present,
Like a beacon on the land,
The magic of the moment,
We must capture in our hand,
For when the sun sets slowly,
When the dusk is closing in,
And when this day is over,
It's too late then, to begin.
So we'll begin tomorrow,
That's when we will stop to see,
That's the time for being present,
That's the time for you and me,
Now tomorrow is today,
Today in yesterday is lost,
In futures and in pasts the years roll by,
Our life, the cost.

Prayer

Pray, and in the praying learn to feel,
Just thinking prayer will never make it real,
Pour out your heart and saturate your soul,
Just talking prayer will never make you whole.
So take the time to visit God each day,
And make the time to go within and pray,
Know, and in the knowing find peace there,
Feel, when'er you visit God in prayer.

A Blessing

May we see with our hearts,
So love shines from our eyes,
May we feel with our souls,
So our hands will be gentle,
May we hear with our very beings,
So we vibrate in harmony
With all living things.

978-0-595-42198-5
0-595-42198-9

CPSIA information can be obtained at www.ICGtesting.com
Printed in the USA
LVOW120735190812

294835LV00003B/9/A